IN THE NAME OF NARID

Andrew Suknaski
IN THE NAME OF NARID

NEW POEMS EDITED BY DENNIS COOLEY

The Porcupine's Quill, Erin, 1981

Copyright © Andrew Suknaski, 1981.

Financial assistance towards publication of this volume has been
received from the Multicultural Program, Secretary of State,
Government of Canada, whose support is gratefully acknowledged.
Published by The Porcupine's Quill, Inc., 68 Main Street, Erin,
Ontario NOB ITO.

Both the author and publisher wish to extend their thanks to
Anna Balan, Chrystyna Hnatiw, Dennis Cooley, Vera Skop, Bohdan
Krawchenko, Andrij Hornjatkevyc, and Jars Balan.

The author is also grateful to the Canada Council.

Designed by Tim Inkster. Printed and bound in an edition of 1,000
copies (March, 1981) by The Porcupine's Quill, Inc. The type is
Stempel Garamond composed at The Coach House Press (Toronto)
and the stock, Zephyr Antique Laid.

Photographs by Harvey Spak.

ISBN 0-88984-037-7

A NOTE REGARDING PRONUNCIATIONS:

All accents, as well as Roumanian and Polish words, are rendered phonetically in English by the poet. Ukrainian words and expressions are transliterated according to the Modified Library of Congress System with the exception of such words as Kiev, Dnieper and cossack, whose English orthography has already been established. The following key of approximate pronunciations is therefore designed to help readers decipher some of the more awkward-looking transliterations encountered in the poems.

a – as in m*a*m*a*	kh – as in Scottish lo*ch*
e – as in *a*pple	zh – as in French *J*ean
y – as in *e*xample	iu – as in *you*
i – as in *ee*l	ie – as in *ye*s
u – as in troops!	ia – as in *ya*cht

Unpronounced Ukrainian soft signs are not indicated in this system. It should also be noted that [y] is used in the plural form of words, one pysanka becoming two pysanky.

Dedicated to the memory of my father and mother.

I am my father's father,
You are your children's guilt
. . . .
Child labour! The child must carry
His fathers on his back.

Delmore Schwartz

AFTER 'A PRAIRIE BOY'S SUMMER'

to the memory of william kurelek

suknatskyj listens
to what the dry grass speaks
in the vernacular   of wind
across prairie
   and who is this sleek cat
   invading   like a memory
   the barnyard   of youth?

who is this cat
a ghost
or some god
meowling litanies
in praise   to earthly residence
   ... a man   and woman
   toiling in kinship
   from sunup
   to sundown?

my God!
the swallow divebombs   the cat
as if the air we breathe
were a territory
to defend

9

під тягарем хреста, прошу Тебе, захорони мене перед усяким упадком в гріх.

Люблю Тебе Ісусе:

Отче наш: Богор. Діво: Слава: І нині:

IV.
Ісус Христос стрічає Страдаючу Свою Матір.

Величаєм Тя, животдавче Христе, і чтем крест Твой честний, імже спасл єси нас от работи вражія.

Розваж, яка була стріча Сина й Матері на тій дорозі болю. Ісус і Марія поглянули взаїмно на Себе, й кілько разів обіймилися поглядом, стільки мечів болю пронило наскрізь їхні люблячі Серця.

Наймиліший Ісусе! Через лютий біль, що Ти його дізнав

KOSMACH

home of valentyn moroz
in moscow's vladimir prison no. 2

Kosmach
      where dream of home
            lies
                curled
      in horns
           of *baran*

         ram
            gracing *pysanka*

     dream of home
            contained

    in the carpathian
         ram
            hutsul symbol
   for leadership
         and strength
   in face of
        adversity

2. HUNGER STRIKE

hutsul pride   and hoping
for survival of country
moroz   today you bid farewell
to your faithful wife
young son
and your father

thin faced
emaciated
and sunken
dark eyes
you said
 'i'm finishing
  myself off'

saying goodbye   you kissed
your son's   thin hand
two guards   jumped you
believing you passed
something   onto him
with your mouth
moroz   they
have always failed
to understand
fear itself
moroz
what they fear most
is the strength
you stand for
the simple love
you pass on
your son   took home
today

WHAT IS REMEMBERED

to the memory of volodymyr ivasiuk 1949-1979

what is remembered
                is remembering
                          what is

the smell of grass on fresh earth
                          just after
                                    the rain
when you are young and swept away
                          that day becoming
                the first time
                          again
          glimmering
                in a blossoming lilac
                                    when wind
                          rises
                          where you are older

what is remembered
                is remembering
                          what was

the first story /
                that levite woman bearing
                          a healthy child
          later hidden
                in a papyrus basket
                          set among
                reeds
                          on the river's edge
the pharaoh's daughter
                sending a maid
                          to fetch it
                someday
                          to be named
                                    moses
                'one drawn
                          from the water'

what is remembered
             is remembering
                          what is

the common hurt
             of parting
                          where the vast river flows on
far beyond those
             who carry
                          fire
                                       and the cry
                                                    'HERE I AM!'
             those impaled
                          on the horns
                                       of a ram
             that must be wrestled
                                       to its death
             those who
                          take refuge in
                                       naming
                                                    the eternal
parable /
             biblical naomi
                          her natural
                                       losses:
             that certain
                          man
                                       two sons
                                                    survived by
             one daughter-in-law
                                       who remains in
                                                    the alien land
                          and another pleading
                                       permission
                                                    to return

14

Wherever you go, I will go.
Wherever you live, I will live.
Your people shall be my people,
and your God, my God.
Wherever you die, I will die
and there I will be buried.

that other one
                known as *ruth*
'the beloved
                companion'
                        who lonely
        gleaned corn
                in still another
                        foreign land

2. MYTH

what is remembered
                is remembering
                        what is

myth / names
        rusalka
                some child dying
                        unnamed
        rusalka
                a female fetus
                        summoned to light by
                a drunkard's
                        boot
        rusalky
                do they ever speak
                        the dead
                                unnamed
                back
                        into life?

15

do they ever see
                    didy
          and *baby*
                         'the ancestors'
        the ghostly
                    plowmen
                              and hoeing women
        shouldering
                         weaver's dream
                                   among the living
                 who work
                              tireless
                                   on the margins
                                             of *selo*?*

didy / *baby*
            some say
                    they are the melting of
                                        snow
                 the arrival
                         of spring
                                   warmth

                 others claim
                         they are
                                   sustaining
                              green things

didy / *baby*
            some tell
                    of glimpsing
                              the peaceful
                         faces
                              shadows
                                        in ripening rye

selo: Ukrainian for village. Also implies a sense of community.

3. REALITY

what is remembered
            is remembering
                    what is

toughs raiding
            across borderland
                        that once was
        krai
            'cut'
                    becoming *ukraina*

                    thugs
                            digging in
                                    like termites

what is remembered
            is remembering
                    what happened

        the great river
                    dniester
                            flowing quietly
                                        the dark
                                undertow

        then that final night
                            in spring
                                    goons deadringing
                for ghouls
                            summoned you
                                        volodymyr
                                                from your conservatory
                    your name
                                redoubled
                                        in dark cadence

                    'VOLODYMYR!
                                VOLODYMYR!'

'THAT IS YOUR NAME
ISN'T IT?'

'What do you want
of me?'

and they, those state slugs,
                    bloated on vodka and blood
         drove you
                  volodymyr
                          to moriah darkness
          of bryukhovychi
                       forest
                            near lviv

what is remembered
                    is remembering
                               what happened

before
         those living their promise
                              of home
                                      in the boundaries
                  of a woman's pain
                              along the river's
                                         edge
                   those immutable things
                               sealed in the blood
                  -bound chronicles /

ivan the terrible
                   first czar of russia
           ivan
               of goat's eyes
                          the model lunatic

in that other land
          forcing famine
                              '31 to '34
          7.0 million
                              metric tons of grain
          exacted
                    from ukraine
          112 kg.
                    grain left
                              for each peasant
          5 to 6
                    million dead in
                              3 years
                    some perishing
                              by cholera
                    some by
                              spotted fever
                                        and dysentry
                         others
                              mostly
                                   by famine
                    some who survived
                              remembering

                    'some washed away
                    by the flood
                    floated down the dnieper
                    ripe ... as mushrooms'

and finally
          there was stalin
                    who paid tribute
          to the last
                    trace
                         of an oral tradition
          by holding
                    the first symposium
                              of *bandurysty*

blind
     crippled
          kozak minstrels
  abounding wine
     platters
          smothered with
    finest
       meats

fêted their rueful *dumas*
        'lyrical
           epics'
  haunting *bandury*
     moving him
        to tears

lifted his right hand and started
        the machineguns'
    clatter ...

what is remembered
    is remembering
       what happened

that you volodymyr
    vanished
       on an april monday
when others were
    falling in love
       or crossing themselves
    before holy
      sights
you volodymyr
    brilliant young
       doctor
   in rufescent
     flowering

"maria! dunia!
have you heard volodymyr's
chervona ruta
'the red ruta-flower'?
his finest song yet!"

you later found
            hanging
                    from a tree
        the official KGB
                    report
                        claiming
                                death by suicide.

volodymyr
        your dark cipher
                        remains
        ... how does one
                        disappear
        one week after
                    easter sunday
                                    to be found
            a week before
                        ascension?

        *It is not for you to know
        times or dates that
        the father has decided
        by his own authority...
        you will be my witnesses
        ... to the ends
        of the earth.*

but tell me
        volodymyr
                how does a suicide
cover his own body
                in lacerations
                            and bruises?

or drive broken branches of
                              the redberried
                kalyna tree
                        through his own ribs
                or climb
                        to tie
                              a rope?

        tell me volodymyr
                        how did you really ascend
                                        the kalyna tree
                whose rueful wood
                        your *didy* and *baby*
                                        hewed
                        into a ladder
                                of enduring
                                        dumy?

what is remembered
                is remembering
                        what is

        unnecessary
                to imagine
                        beyond
        the first
                grim act /

        "'*so* maestro!
        you're the famous composer
        are you?
                        very well then ...'

                'HOLD DOWN HIS HANDS
                ON THAT STONE THERE!
                FINE'

'*now* maestro
play your great *kozak* opera
for your God
when you arrive'

what is remembered
                    is remembering

to ponder
            the final question /
why
        would a suicide choose
                        a forbidden military zone
to pluck out his own eyes
                    like notes erased
                                from a music sheet?

    i suppose your assassins
                        volodymyr
                                feared
            bob dylan
                and joan baez
                            in your songs
perhaps
        it was the smell of tight
                        new *levis*
        some herbal dream
                    pillowed
                            on balsam thighs
        nudging
                every stanza
                        that haunted

            partyline metaphor
                            or that other country
            turning
                    the simple lyric
                                into dayold
                    mashed
                            potatoes

perhaps it was only
                the absence
                        in your art
  of some nightmare utopia
                  latticed in ozone shadows
                              of sheol
        where lenin and stalin
                rule
                  fording a river
                        of blood

what is remembered
            is remembering
                  what is

the ordinary fate
                of suffering servants
those gazing
            through the glass
                  darkly
those who
           must witness
                the others
        who sleep
            dream
                their thin bodies slit open
       never to rise
             from the riverbed
those sleepless
            on the margins of *dumy*
                  still
            as berries
                on a dry autumn branch
                        motionless
          till a sudden wind
                passes

each *dumka*
            'thought'
                        fading
like the harmonic
            signature
                        of a blind *banduryst*
his *bandura* angled
                        away
                                    from wind
            that became
                        a song
                                    to live again
                        in carved
                                    wood
                                                of a new land

wherever you go
volodymyr
wherever the vast
river
            flows on

            we go
            with you

wherever we live
you live
            with us
            all these things
            wherever there is
            ample love
            to will them
                        back into life
                        volodymyr

the photograph arrives
three months after suknatskyj's mother   has died
with it   a letter
suknatskyj cannot read
the place is a poor home
where his mother was born
in the photograph   a middleaged man lies
in a simple coffin   and stapled to wood
is black cloth   trimmed with white ferns
a printed text   reading
SPOCZNEK WIECNY
wiecny 'forever   eternal'
the only word
suknatskyj   understands

    Dear Andrei,

      First, I want to tell you that,
    I was very surprised when I've got a
    letter from you. I have expected a
    letter from my sister Julia. When the
    letter was delivered and I saw a
    photo copy I knew, that my sister died,
    and she will never write to me.
    In first minute I could not believe that
    it is true, that I haven't a dear Julia,
    that she is not alive.

in the photograph   he lies with hands
folded in prayer
a rosary threaded   through them
the ten mourners are all strangers   to suknatskyj
except for the elderly lady   on the far left
the lady looking so much   like suknatskyj's mother
must be his aunt maria
beside the head   of the dead man
a yellow candle   burns

*Now, I sometimes think about my
Canadian family and I can not understand
why you, or anyone with family, didn't
come to Poland so far. You have a big
family in our country. In Poland lives
my youngest sister Emilia. She wrote
letters to your mother too.*

suknatskyj lost   in revery
... eleven strangers to me
yet were she living   beyond her bluegreen eyes
blurring   she would silently name them all
their names orbiting   the yellow cross
in her memory ... name them all
from other photographs   and letters
remembered

*In former times I had a hope, that I
would see Julia or anyone from my
Canadian family. Now, when she isn't
alive, I've lost hope. Andrei, your
mother often wrote me about you.
I will be very happy when I can see
you in Poland, in my home.
What do you think about it?*

Your aunt Maria

suknatskyj   turning the photograph
vertically
             ... stand dead man
             stand stranger
             a moment
             in those brand new shoes
             laced   on your dead feet
             new shoes   for your long journey
             ... stand dead man
             and let the mourners   lie
             while i read your face more
             oriental   than anything
             your face   still brown
             and burnished
             by faraway sun   and suffering
             your face forged   by all things
                  chinese
                  tartar
                  hutsul
                  viking
                          cossack horsemen
                  who forded   the rivers
                  of your frozen
                  blood

dear mykola

    dearr? *shcho vam za dilo?*
    vhat cohncerrn eez eet   off yourz?

peace   mykola
sheathe your tongue   a moment!
i'll address you as i wish
mykola   your granddaughter
who no longer believes in salutations
or formal endings to letters
bears the loneliness
of your absence
mykola   do you know she still searches for you
departed from this earth   at 35?

spokii! peace!   mykola
time no longer presses into your face
and i am older than you now
the search   mykola
that mad slavic compulsion!

    '*I will never   never give up*
    till I find that place
    all I want   is to place
    a tombstone there
    in his memory'

you know mykola   my father
homesteaded on canadian prairie
the year you arrived   in america

mykola   on a sleepless new york city night
your granddaughter   wrote a letter
arriving on my 36th birthday

'I had to see the city
that didn't hear my grandfather's pain
that appleblossom night   in 1914.
He had fled to America
a dream needling his brain.
And I returned to miss him
in the archives' dust.
There is no photograph of him   anywhere.'

mykola   how does one just vanish
from ships' lists
stored in a computer's   memory bank
in one's port of entry?

mykola   it would be so easy
if you were the only one
but there was someone before you
and the record only hints
at the strange features
of that face   its light
pulling paul   blinded
to his knees
that other face
a light knocking the breath out of
tereasa de jesús   speechless

mykola   a man called jorge luis borges
claims that's the way
it was meant to be   that other man
faceless   that God might become
all of us

i don't know   mykola
i wonder   do any of us
ever ascend to margins where things
become a human face?
what do we do with the unknown
philosophical farmer
that old ukrainian   in manitoba
leaving behind

a diary and a second edition   of DILO
a newspaper published in lviv
november 14th   1933
two columns   on the right side
of page one   blanked out
the story gone
plate photo   and type
lifted out   to satisfy a censor's whim
no one out there   must see these
thin faces   chronicling the homeless
and cholera   7½ million dead
in those years of famine
forced by russia

mykola   what does one make
of the cyrillic irony
at the bottom   of that blank space?

'1000 invalids from the Ukrainian
Army of Halychyna await the
community's aid. Honour their
achievements and dedication.
The dignity of a people demands
a guarantee of life for those
who gave up their health
in defence of their homeland.'

what does one make   of the next page
the simple   cyrillic plea
on the margins of a white space

SPREAD OUR WORD!

God   mykola
what do we make
of all these sad things?

                    liubov,
                        Andrei Suknatskyj

p.s. mykola   last night
        i touched the soft light   on the edge
        of your granddaughter's face
        and you knuckling the pane
        33 stories above a park
        did not allow her   or me
        any sleep ...

    32

IX.
Ісус падає третій раз під тягарем хреста.

Величаєм **Тя**, животдавче Христе, і чтем крест **Т в о й** честний, імже спасл єси н а с от работи вражія.

Розваж. як Ісус третій раз падає під хрестом, бо був дуже обезсилений, а жорстокі кати мимо того силували Його, щоби прискорив ходу, коли Він вже ледви крок вперед міг поступити.

О так немилосердно мучений мій Ісусе! Через заслуги Твоїх з'усиль, які Ти добровільно зносив в дорозі на Голгофту, благаю Тебе, скріпи мене таким запалом, щоб я вже більше не оглядався на люд...

WEST TO TOLSTOI, MANITOBA (CIRCA 1900)

the story of the young ukrainian immigrant
imprisoned   in his language and ghetto
his name no longer remembered
but an aging woman in assiniboia
tells the rest about him
spending those lonely winters in montreal with nothing
but a friend's letters from tolstoi
ukrainian hamlet in rural manitoba
whitewashed   straw and mud shacks
with thatched roofs
the way it was done   in the homeland

others who relate the story   are not certain
how many times he left montreal on foot
each spring
with never more than a couple dollars change in his pocket
and how he always followed   the railway tracks west
stopping at some station   to check a map
to see where he was
occasionally helped   by some station agent
who offered food   and a bed
hassled by railway officials
who always failed to understand his talk
and sent him   back on an eastbound train
free

no one knows   how far he got each time
until one year   he met some ukrainian immigrants
at a station   in central ontario
where he embraced one of them   and told his story
'please   take me with you
i never   want to speak
to another englishman
for the rest of my life'

35

suknatskyj's father remembering

syrota   she an herr fahderr
dey leef long ago   een karpateh
she noh heveh mahderr
pohany   vaz pagenz!

fahderr vent vay somverr vonc
dey vahzzeh verry poorr
he vent vay vorrk   forr vile
sommeh nunz   dey commeh geev herr food
starrtink tell err bout chrrist
all deem storry

fahderr commeh bek hom
ketch herr prrayink
he starrt   beatink herr
tole herr   forrget evrrytink
nunz telleh herr
she say   'noh!'
she be likkeh dem beauteeful storry
soh he putteh lohgz een fireplec
ven good firre goink
he drehggeh herr crross florr
'you noh stahpeh behleevink
i troh you een firre!'
she noh frraid   noh say nhotiink
he putteh herr clohc to flemz
she feeleh nohtink
he trroh herr   crross florr

nextteh he boilink beeg pot   bearr fet
den he tekkeh herr by hairr
'you stahpeh behleevink
all dem storry   oh i troh you een!'
she say 'noh!'
he putteh herr een   nohtink heppin
she noh crryeh
by ghalley   he tekkeh heez ehx

datzzeh be da firrc   syrota
orrphan chile

37

late winter
he journeys from calgary   to saskatoon
to see a daughter   and her children
then rides the greyhound down to regina
where his celibate son
will pick him up
and drive him out to the farm

in the front seat
he and suknatskyj   gaze at the breathsweeping   blue sky
cornelius   enjoying the day
with one good eye
speaks

   "the dneiper ... it is as blue as the sky out there
   i remember it perfect
   perfect   clear blue water   me
   and my boyhood friends   swam in
   my home town was
   nyzhnakhortytsia ... khortytsia
   that's the 'she skunk'
   anyway   we would walk along the river
   to some pools near big stones
   they called *porohy*
   there were rapids there
   but we swam in the pools   downstream a bit
   beautiful water
   crystal clear water ...
   you walked out of the water
   and just brushed the sand   off your feet
   anyway   down from the pools
   was the village named   *zaporohy*
   my town   *nyzhnakhortytsia*
   was just across the dneiper
   from there
     ... and just down the river from there
     up on the hillside

there were some other stones
just like *porohy*   and on one of them
stood a huge sculpture   of taras bulba
in our country then
we always chose a hill like that
for a monument   always
because at the back of our mind
we always had clear image
of *mohyla*
'the hill'   where the hero
lies buried"

cornelius tells of his blind saskatoon daughter
who teaches braille
his right   workswollen fingers
now a feminine white
delicately move across aluminum rivets
just under the window
as though trying   to decode
some cipher   or mystery there

in the other dead eye   lingers
the memory   of a steel splinter
that darkened the blue   july sky
40 years ago
on his farm

cornelius confirms
    "yes ... village is *selo*
        if you were walking somewhere
        and you saw a place
        maybe   a church steeple rising   to the blue sky
        you thought ... *selo!*
        see people there   had spirit
        and strength
                ... any other place
                without that
                was *dereva*
                'dead trees!'"

for george morrissette

sidestreets   surrounding *prosvita* hall
vanished with games
cowboys an indians   and *run sheep run*
became prairie   for him   and his playmates

cattle   bellowing   death's cold inklings
in the stockyard   across the tracks
were his buffalo
slaughter houses   spewing guts' steam
shacks   his hills
where trapped gods   sent smoke signals
a boy could read
while sledding   spumed rapids
in a river of stars
on a winter's   steelcold night

on a friday night   when friends fled
to the warm hutch   of home
wailing fiddles   drew him   from the lonely
st boniface street
and he would quietly sneak   into that hall
teeming   with laughter
another people   still not his own
they speaking a language
he could never comprehend
held by some mystery
where the small   tired children
slept   on wooden benches
he would wistfully gaze   at dancers
tirelessly dancing   to all those slavic tunes
so haunting   and unlike
anything   his metis stepfather
teased   from a cracked fiddle
and there   he dreamed

someday   one day
i'll play fiddle
'the devil's dream'
jus like them old men
bless their gypsy souls!

a man later   cursed
by the bastard's search   for home
he slowly   learns all
old fiddle tunes   remembered
clear enough   that gypsy joy
glimmering beyond   slavic soul
never be   mistaken   for anything else
until metis fiddle   and gypsy
slavic fiddle   become a single spirit
shouldering   the soundpeg
beneath   wooden structure
where ghosts dance   'the devil's dream'

he remembers it all   that small hall
a certain   beginning
in that place
with a slavic   name
prosvita

for j.n.

dear john
    i'm sendin you a contact print
from some photographs   found in the album
of an 80 year old widow
my mother shared a house with her
a few winters   in assiniboia
told me about her recent fall
spoke of kneelin among scattered
japanese oranges   down in the cellar

  'lohrra ... lohrra
  how deed you   get herre lohrra?'

mother cradled the frail   small woman
like a child   in her arms
tried to rock her awake
                anyway
these photos john   i donno
donno why i send em
wonder if you've ever seen em
think it's mostly something to do
with the bottom of stairways
where our lives   cross
                anyway   the story is
your mother an laura   taught at tolstoi
manitoba   1916
their school house   was called *chervona*
'the red one'
they shared a thatched roof   teacherage
an after they went   their separate ways
they always wrote letters
                i remember
the old widow sayin   that last time

'when she married
an had her first son
she sent me this photograph
she sometimes wrote
about those years
often nothing   but bread
potatoes an tea
on the table'

that one photograph   john
your mother   a beautiful young
woman then   hair combed   straight an simple
a single lock   covering her right eye
an curving down   to meet smile
forever there   over her son
sleeping in the carriage
where one can almost smell   the lilac hedge
bordering the crunch   of gravel walk
and the long dress she wears
brightening   those black shoes
that mirror the sky
                    anyway   john
i'm sendin you this print
an keepin one for myself
pinned directly   above a family photo
me standin against the lilacs
on my sixth birthday   before we all left
the farm an father   for good
                            i send you these
prairie icons   for the possible
poem   they may unlock

                    take care,
                    suknatskyj

43

dear andrei

never before have i seen a picture of my mother
at that age   i loved her
but we couldn't talk
our family never did
she was a beautiful woman
who lived a very difficult life
i think i'm about ready to   you'll
have to write the poem
i can't

j.

44

tulova
      that final peace
            with spirit
      and earth

she naming it
      after that *selo*
            her parents left
      in *ukraina*

she buying it
      with hardearned
            writer's money
   remembering
      the sacrifice
         it took
   to turn horizon
      and forest
         into something
     of remembered
        steppes

it is noon
     in late summer
          where shadows lengthen
   when she
      and good friend
         suknatskyj
  stand
    arm on shoulder
        arm on waist
  among tall
     corn stalks
       on the margins
    of sunflowers
       bright yellow
   and dark
      brown heads splayed
           against
        blue
         sky

... that ancient
    daguerrotype
       like a bush burning
  in the memory
     of men
      and all women

that other woman
      kneedeep
        and alone
    in a field
      of alien grain
  she in revery
     weaving thoughts
        through
          centuries

'... small feet   and hands
have still not swum
in my sea
               tiny elbows
have still not
bruised my womb
                    movements
of flesh and bone
swaddled in luminous dreams
have still not become
a moth's wings
                    brushing the spine
               of that man
               my other self
               sleeping
                         with his back
               to me

               i donno
                    ... he vanished
                    all too soon'

in the evening
          blood red *borshch*
                    savoured
          and the last crust
                    of bread
                         broken

3. MARX' WOMAN

she hands suknatskyj
                her rifle

'try that tin can
on the barn windowsill
gun's ready   jus flip it off *safty*
the red dot   should be showing'

PTZWWWAAAaaaaaaaannnnnnnnng!

    on the garden's edge
                the sunflowers stand
                          motionless
          like a firing squad
                  behind her

left of the window
          where a poster engraving
                    is pinned
   to the crumbling wall
          karl marx
     winces
          frowning at the hopeless
                     marksmanship
       of suknatskyj

'myrna   can i try agen?'

    'jus keep squeezin the trigger
    there are 12 more'

'mhuuu ... guss sleepin with this
thing   by your bed   summer nights
you don't really have to worry
about any strange wackos
comin round'

    'never'

LEBRET MISSION / QU'APPELLE

for myrna kostash

spring
                three years now when gimli's odin
                                                she and suknatskyj
                walked the clearing
                                        by trembling aspens
                and saw
                        a young man revving a honda
                                                slowly ascending
                        the stations of the cross
                                                beneath the mission

suknatskyj remembers
                                her amazing dark eyes
                                                w i d e n i n g
                her face
                        flattening
                                in dismay

                remembers something
                                        freezing her there

today suknatskyj
                        notes the luna moth
                                                resting
                from all her journeys
                                she now sleeping
                                                in the first
                        morning sun
                                        where she
                                                clings
                        to the screen
                                        of the east window
                                                        down from
                                        the mission

suknatskyj remembers
                    how he once caught one
                                        kept her
                    captive
                            in a small
                                        clear container
and then
            on a summer evening
                            baited a hook
casting her
            far to a dark pool
                            among deadwoods
            of a mountain
                            lake

        remembers
                    the wide circles
                                she beat
                    with her
                            soft wings
                                    the way
                    they moved out
                                through mirrored
                    stars
                            when the great
                                        bulltrout
                            rose through
                                        orion
                            to crush her

50

remembers
          standing there
                         gently touching
her delicate
          head
                a moment
          she
                scarcely stirring
before
      stapling
                down to wood
the moving
          window screen

          sleep   peacefully
          woman   dreams
          heal you
                    from your long
                    journey

for glen sorestad

sorestad at the wheel
as the car bucks   the cold morning wind
5 AM   saturn   above southern hills
two hours to scout lake   and sunrise
the hunters talk very little
smoke   comfortable in the quiet
language of plains   and ancestors
the sleepheavy silence   nudges thoughts closer
to something very old   painted shadows
flaking from   walled memory

two sage hens   sighted in pinto horse butte country
the week before   still softly trample
the frosted stubble   in suknatskyj's memory
like gods forsaken

sorestad murmurs 'got any matches on you?'
suknatskyj   hands him a wooden match
they light up   gazing out over southern prairie
where orion   is a kite
some chinese boy flies   in a dream
on the other side   of the world

sunrise   approaching scout lake
suknatskyj tells sorestad   of kerrila buccatar
living in the corner   of the hamlet
   'las time   at sunrise   when gallagher
   marty   and i   came this way
   kerrila was shaving in that window there
   likely gettin ready   to take a bus to assiniboia
   for his monthly gallon of wine
   when ee still lived back in wood mountain
   the roumanian kids an i   used to call im *bahbok*
   the word for duckling   in roumanian'
turning right   they drive up into   high hills
above the scout lake
both only   an eye now
they spot a covey of partridge

knowing this late in the season   birds are spooked
only sorestad shoots   a miss
and the covey wings far down   into the coulee
seeking refuge   on the edge of the hamlet
suknatskyj wonders   if the shot   disturbed *bahbok's* sleep
he maybe   drowsily mumbling to himself
what he called children   back in wood mountain
bahbokolie!

late afternoon   driving the north and west gridroads
through vasile tonita's farmland
and on to   the abandoned sidorick farm
the hunters stop   by the old house   and gate
where a sign   has been hung   on a single barbed wire

NO TRESPASSING

jip   a 17 year old dog   slowly emerges
from the poplars   suknatskyj   calls him
    'JIP ... HERE JIP'
jip doesn't come   as he used to
remembers suknatskyj and gallagher   the week before
he keeps his distance   suknatskyj thinking
    if jip could only speak   he would have told baba
    the full story   the day she came out nostalgic
    from assiniboia   to bathe   his neck wound
    limping away   he would have muttered
    'that goddamn fuckin suknatskyj
    he an some friend of his   an this big black
    huntin dog   they always come tramplin
    through the garden   lookin for pheasants
    i watched them las week
    till that sly black var'iat   *'that bastard'*
    jumped me
                anyway   that asshole poet suknatskyj
                was good enough to come
                an kick the himno   *outta that black* didko
                chewin my neck   while i squirmed
                on my back'

suknatskyj tells sorestad   to shut the motor off
and tries once more
   'JIP ... HERE JIP
   COME ON BOY!'   jip doesn't move
              only looks their way   a moment
              before fading   back into poplars

when the car starts up   a cock and hen
swiftly rise from the tall weeds
in the corner   of the garden   and fly far beyond
the house

the hunters drive on   suknatskyj glimpses   jip
still watching from the trees   the lonely place
  so much   fled
  from my   slavic memory

for the sorestads

suknatskyj no longer favouring the back
sits right in front
the bus bucking the great north wind
to saskatoon
suknatskyj bushed again
in the hutch of urban despair
and fleeing   across prairie
that becomes an incurable need
at least twice a year

suknatskyj nods into revery
where snow sifts   across cold pavement
while the bus driver struggles to keep awake
under the blizzard's hypnosis

> *... somewhere in another century*
> *in another country*
> *a young girl walks leaning into storm*
> *to take refuge*
> *among pear trees*
> *near home*
> *and somewhere deep in her mind*
> *a dido sings*

> > 'orphan ... orphan
> > are you made of snow
> > or frost
> >   moroz   is that
> >   what makes you   so cold?'

> > *the song's orphan child*
> > *replying:*

> > > 'dido ... dido
> > > i am not snow   or frost
> > > only tears!'

suknatskyj drowsing in the gathering storm
remembers   baba's story
how she never *did* hear
the end of the song   looming
in her transylvanian dream
or in the new land   another home
where she fled to weep
in nearby willows
returning only when her father
came home   from work

suknatskyj somewhere between sleep and dream
where forms assume
a ghostly density

  ... a new home
  another decade
  a scantily dressed girl searching
  in storm   for the lost
  horses ...

where a ghostly voice
is murmuring

  'she lost all her toes
  to frostbite   that time
  13   when she ran away from home
  some home   with that miserable bitch
  of a stepmother
  anyway   an old neighbor woman
  took her in
  baba stayed there a couple years
  then went to work as a waitress
  in moose jaw
  lived in a rooming house where dido was
  another guy there proposed to her
  an she said to him

'ia kalika! *i'm crippled*
but if you want me
you'll have to take me
the way i am   kalika!'

well i guess the guy wasn't too much interested
in a woman   with no toes
so he shied away
anyway   dido came along
an she told him the same thing
they married a few weeks later
then headed south   to the homestead
an you know baba   she was 77 this year
went up to buchanen this summer
with sister mary
they asked some ole ukrainian farmer
about that woman
who took baba in that time
the ole guy pointed across a field

   '*she lives right over there*'

when the woman opened the door
baba whispered   her name

   '*laura*'

well my God! that ole woman embraced her
nearly crushing baba's back

   'syrota ... *my child!*
   why did you wait   so long?'

a wind blast rocks the bus
while suknatskyj wakens   to remember
baba's bitter words

57

'vhat ees to say now?
dhat sohn een law
on heez brrahderr
dido vahz alvays call dhem
tasyhany!   geepsiez!
dhat sohn een law
dido vahz say bout heem
'he deeg myne grrave
an he fall een et heemself!'
dido vahz say dhat
afterr funerral
on die von veek laterr
i'm sohrry forr boht now
eetz all ohverr   dhat hating
on now dhat sohn frrom ceety
leefink vife
on runnink roun veet nahdderr von
las veek she an mahderr veet heem
pohkink nohz roun farrm
vhat me an dido slayfink forr all deez yearz
i tole dhat sohn
'you got not von
but two *kurvy* now!
two *kurvy*!'
dhat be mine life herre now
like dhat *syrota*
dhat orrphan child
ohnly tearrz!
crryink boat dhay an night
ohnly tearrz!'

suknatskyj tired and hungry
weary of aloneness
while the bus wheels into the new concrete depot
looming in the storm
like a fortress
suknatskyj rising in the evening light
a passing thought

58

you enjoy baba's bitter tea
and say

     dobranich!
     'good evening!'

you do not feign a kiss
on baba's purple lips
soft   as lilacs

and she embraces you
the way a strong northern wind hugs
a cornerpost
on the flat
prairie

after linocut by george melnyk

suknatskyj's mother   savouring black current wine
he has squirreled away   for 8 years
she gazes at the print
on his shack's wall
asks what it is

too long from home
and unable   to speak ukrainian
the way he used to
he cannot translate   his friend's title

    the land also rises

so suknatskyj tells her
    'paska i khmary'
                easter bread   and clouds

    studying details
    she asks
           'vhat be dhat underr clouds?'

                'polia
                   … fields'
                          he murmurs
              'navit polia
                  v nebi
              even fields in
                    heaven'

she finishing wine
to add
        'orr myte be rrayz ov sohn
        ahbofh cloudz   brroken
        by geese   koming norrt
        yah   i see
        nice day today
        might you be deek   myne garrden?'

leaving home again
        suknatskyj knows
                it will not be easy
     in the darkening avenue
           of memory
  is fully aware
       there'll be no
            absolute forgetting
  that thursday night
        burning grass
             in the church yard
      that evening
         of good intentions
 or wakening
      from deep sleep
          on the sofa
     the whole living room
            glowing
               red
  his terrified mother
       framed
         by the doorway
     struggling
      for breath

     'the choorrch
     the choorrch eez burrnin
     poorr ... churrch'

never will suknatskyj forget
        the vaulting
           pyramidal flames
  his heart rising on
      bitter tide
 people gathering
      to stand helpless

swollen with spring
                    runoff
the cold thoughts

never will suknatskyj forget
                    the whole edifice crumbling
    to the foundation
                his whole mind
                        numb

    the bell
            tumbling
                to   CLANG!
                        on the concrete
                                hallway

            yes   you
            who were so *certain*
            the evening dew
            had strangled   every spark

    the great bell
                glowing
                        red
                            in the embers

suknatskyj's mother
                    next day
                            she kneading tears
        into bittersweet
                    dough
                        she braids
                                in lonely thought

gone myne choorch
wherre i vahshed floorrs
on myne kneez   forr tventy yearrz
gone gold crross
chahleec   an candlesteeks
i ahlvayz pahleeshed
teel i saw myne face
gone iconz

his broken mother
                suddenly there
                                like a visitation
                from some charred
                                village
                                        in the ukraine

she knuckling
                the burnt broom
                                in her right hand

            'vehrr verr you burrning
            lahss nite?
                        tell me
                        vehrr?'

                                stony silence
                only sounds
                            of the old priest
                                        beyond caraganas
                where he ambles in ruins
                                        retrieving
                            candlesticks
                                chains
                                        and incenseburners.

            "eet vahss you
            you veel pay forr dheec
            'pohanyn' ..."

the schoolchildren
                    at recess
                                ringing the grey bell
          with small stones
                    flung from the road

suknatskyj saying
                    goodbye
                              to his mother
          who does not
                    face him

                              only stretches out
                                        her left hand

                              'tek dhis lohf   easterr brread
                              myte you be get   hahgrry
                              vehrr you   goink'

suknatskyj
          on a northbound
                              bus
          where the dark
                    window
                              mirrors
          nothing
                    moving alone
                              in thoughts
                    of home
                              and sleep

64

DOMINION DAY DEPARTURES

julia suknatskyj (1899-1978)

north of lac la ronge
                a saturday
                              clear blue sky
  stanley mission road
                  suknatskyj
                            back in boyhood magic
  tries to snare a pike
                with wire loop
                        and willow
  when two young
                native women
                            going west in an old hack
                stop

                  'hey   you seen an ole woman
                  come by here?
                  woman wit fishin pole?'

  'no   i've only bin here
  bout an hour   why?'

                  'she wen west   dis way
                  yesserday   never come back'

suknatskyj
        fishing again
                  in niggling cold of morning

on the third day
            late night
                   suknatskyj returning
  to the city
        to find note
                on door

PHONE LEE BACK HOME — IMMEDIATELY.
PEOPLE HAVE BEEN LOOKING FOR YOU
SINCE FRIDAY NIGHT.

EVAN

descends the long stairway
                    walks past lush lilacs
next to the greening
                    caraganas

                    'friday night   tomorrow
                    10 o'clock'

'thanks   sorry to wake you up
goodnight'

> *no longer her thoughts*
> *of all those lone years   back on the farm*
> *ghosts in a wind   forever*
> *curling around eaves that sigh*
> *like lost souls dreaming*
> *no more the memory   of her rasping speech*
> *long after she went away*
> *no more whatever*
> *changed her*
> *children forever*

> > *her slavic prayers   kept her*
> > *her easter litany   kept her*
> > *the firerazed church*
> > *across the street   kept her*

the bright sun   hot
in the garden of summer
and bare feet   in the damp warm earth
kept her
hers now   that last wish
to lie near the corner   of the village cemetery
find vast sleep   within the triangle
the eternal partridge covey   flies

under high sun
                of the windless day
                                the river flows on
    suknatskyj rises
                to ascend the steep path
                                        back to his refuge

    moving alone
                in his black
                        flowering

67

THE GIFT

though some suspect
the old metis woman
south of town
no one is really certain
who it was
        but the gift
        ... a jar
        of sweet water
        containing
        a handful of lilacs
                was there
                on the western edge
                of the open grave
                long before
                suknatskyj's mother was
                buried
                midmorning

GENESIS

long before the word
or someone   to hear it

the garden grows
furred   and taloned things   endure eating

long after naming
dreams   of lineage

the garden grows
south   of sun

and north   of the hands   that seed it
far beyond

the paleo-ikons of the cave
and colourd   runes

easter eggs
hidden   in the grass

the garden grows   high
above the old hands

that seeded
with care   laying it out

in the subtle   precision
of a rembrandt   painting

69

PYSANKY

she gone now
            leaving three
                        pysanky
        in a fruit jar

one mantled by
            prussian blue
                        night
            alive
                with stars

    white lines binding bud
                    and leaf
                            to ferns
                    rooted
                            in dark heaven

            a yellow cross
                        adrift
                near four
                        moons

another
        deep purple
                    space
    graced by
            white
                    green
        and yellow
                runes
                        suknatskyj
                                cannot
                    decipher

the final one
        darker than
                transylvanian
          myth

a single yellow scrawl
            half cross
      half white
         barb
           clinging
    to dense
        night
           the final
     pysanka
        a sign
            though nothing
                works out

KISTKA

wooden splinter
                the edges
                        shaved away
        with a paring
                knife
                        to make

the stylus handle   twice the length
and thickness   of a wooden match

in the split
                end
                        a fragment
of soft metal
                curled
        into
                a tiny cylinder
                                strung with
                black thread
                                down to white
                binding
                        tightly

72

suknatskyj trying
        to imagine
            his mother
      parsnipthick
          fingers
     delicately
         crafting it
     to colour
        those *pysanky*

angular designs
       a web
to catch
    rainbow
       and stars
    barbed
      in boyhood
         memory

73

suknatskyj's father's father   back in the old country
whenever he was plagued by birds   ravaging the garden
he always built *perepolokh* 'scarecrow'
magical word   for any ukrainian youth
perepolokh 'to scare something'
'to blow through   or clear over something'
pere   po   lokh   there was sound
and poetry   in the word   and if you had frightened horses
it was 'rozpolokhani koni' that galloped away   whinnying

suknatskyj's father   now in his 87th year
small sparrows discover the two rows of wheat
and row of flax   he plants each year
on the edge of the garden   since leaving the farm
wheat blended with winter cereal   for body strength
flax for a medicine   mixed with local herbs
in a strong tea

once again   he builds *perepolokh*
his father's old sayings   braided like easterbread   in his memory
leavening
    'ah ole dido   beginning to wander an ramble
    we ought to prop him up   in the garden
    where he can be of some use   *didoperepolokh!*
    a good place too   for nattering ole baba
    where she can beat her gums
    at crows   *babaperepolokh!*'

soon *perepolokh* is ready
neighboring widows laugh   at motheaten overalls
tattered shirt   and hat
while the innocent sparrows   harvesting sweet   hard wheat
don't even notice   *perepolokh!*
old man suknatskyj   goes to the house
finds a dress   his new woman has discarded
pulls it over   *didoperepolokh*
the voluminous   brightflowered dress
waving like a flag   in the wind

cuts his wheat   and flax   with a knife
ties three sheaves   and tucks them
under th hem of the dress
   'there   that'll do the trick   *babaperepolokh*
   will protect em!'
he retreats to the house   brews some coffee
and celebrate's the day's work
a while later   goes outside   to inspect
can't believe his eyes   no wind
and yet   there seem movements   under the dress
suddenly   the sparrow's song   and women's
cackle   reaches him
he runs to *babaperepolokh*   salvages remains
takes the sheaves   into the basement
for further ripening

hearing the story   in some other town
his former wife   reveals a faint   trace of jealousy
   'huh   dhese canadian burds
   dhey not be   so stupid'
young suknatskyj   only smiles

75

andrew suknatskyj (1889-1978)

> *Andrew Suknatskyj*
> *born April 4, 1891*
> *Lemberg, Galicia, Poland.*
>
> *Entered Canada*
> *May 23, 1912.*
>
> *Certificate No. 12620 / series 'A'*
> *Nationalization*
> *June 23, 1921.*

suknatskyj jr
                returning home another fall
                                                to make peace
        with presences
                        lingers by the tall sunflower
        father
                following the sun
                                to another place
        were you as tall
                        as this
                                sunflower?

        father   where did you lose
        or gain   those three years?

        are you really only   the two men
        you sometimes seemed to be?

            silence
                    the splayed shadows
                                    reveal nothing

father   the 10 crisp 100's
you sewed in your underwear
next to your heart
while you prayed for death
as reprieve   from insomnia
... did you actually believe
you might use it
for some eternal homestead?

speak to me sunflower
raise your sleepfilled head

suknatskyj standing
                 frozen
                         by the sunflower
and hollyhock
             remembers a neighbour
                            in the silence

'*the sunflower*
it was the only one that grew
this summer
it didn't bear any seeds
... the hollyhock
it jus grew one year
it never flowered
this summer

          your mother
          was havin these pains
          in her chest
          but insisted on finishing the garden
          one day   the pain was too much
          and she got helen
          to plant the last two rows
          of poppies'

suknatskyj leaving
                    to pause
                              on the garden's eastern edge
          left hand
                    brushes a dry poppy pod
                                        the seeds rattle

            remembers seeing his father
                                        that last time
                    in the hospital
                                        he beyond speech

                    what does it mean
                    his right hand extended
                    rosary tangled
                    in those gnarled fingers?
                    does he know i've lost my faith?
                    has he himself
                    lost faith?
                    and tells me there is only
                    the futility of prayer
                    or is it simply
                    one last   gift?

        remembers
                    that lonely silence
                                        threading it through
                    the left hand's
                                fingers
                                        before returning it

                    'no father   i think it's
                    best you keep it
                    with you'

remembers
        chiding the younger sister
               before the funeral

      'my God   he was a cobbler once
      we can't bury im shoeless
      can't have im walkin barefooted someday
      across stony fields
      Christ! i'll buy im a pair right now
      myself'

     'no   they can't puttem on now
     his feet   would have to be broken'

suknatskyj
      remembers the funeral
                taking the old crucifix
   where his father fastened
            the falling Christ
                 with a red ribbon
    recalls
       one dry poppy pod
             and some
     braided sweetgrass
          under the ribbon
    then slipping
       the crucifix
          into his father's suit pocket

      sleep well
      i'll be around some night
      with a paira shoes

mahzahkazah whiskeylonely   once again on his way
across golgotha prairie   to winnipeg
young balding head   humming electric
with oletime fiddle tunes   he slowly falling asleep
at the wheel   to dream

> *man   man dat muddah fuckin fiddle man!*
> *idda jumped off dat*
> *maddah fuckin brooklyn bridge man   centuries ago!*
> *if it wassin foh that fiddle*

mahzahkahzah nodding   to dream of his female jewish
new york psychiatrist   who once advised
   'love your metis stepparents   you must
   but remember   you are white
   and their world   is not yours
   your salvation lies in the green army   tin box
   your stepmother   keeps the adoption papers in
   you must find out   who your real parents are
   you'll never be happy   or know where you belong
   unless you do that!'

> AYYYYYYYE! WAKE UP!
> WATCHDATDHEREDITCHMAN!

mahzahkahzah   who in several hours
will be stopping again   at the same gulf station
owned by a greying   man in east kildonan
mahzahkahzah   uncertain
   'filler up please ...'
being very careful   as always   never to say 'father'
mahzahkahzah   who will continue
another 34 blocks   into st boniface
to his metis   wheelchaired stepfather
in a house   forever home   and share with him
a few more   intravenoused years

and then there is suknatskyj
who   in a time of difficult love
grows more fond each day   of the young *aircanada* woman
where home is fixed   in the immutable coördinates
taken by the first power stars   orion
north star   southern cross
over cities pulsing   in the veins   of journeying earth
suknatskyj growing more fond of her   for there can be no other way now
far beyond yellowrange poplars   on the garden's edge
of boyhood memory
    a young woman cries
    as she digs
    a small hole
    with a coalpail shovel
    and a young man returns   from the straw barn
    to hear   and see her
    he going over   to console her
    'dohnt crry ... dohnt crry
    dehrr vill be ahderrz ...'
    he holding her close
    where they kneel

suknatskyj now far beyond   where deeper still
in chlorophylled   boyhood memory
a father tears legs   and heads
from christmas eve dolls
while the family sleeps
severs them   one by one
before casting them all   into the heater
suknatskyj now far beyond   another time
where the heater lid   is slightly open
the firebox's light   becoming bright crescents
embracing shadows   along the ceiling
where a rolling pin   eclipses both
the straight razor   and the axe
while tartar horsemen
still ford   the rivers of
slavic blood

suknatskyj far beyond
the moon
holding a baby's
death certificate
indecipherable
while the wind turns the late
grocer's death ledger
page by page
in the nuisance ground
where something dark
cries through earthfilled
mouth

'MAMO! TATU!   MAMO

                    PETER!

OUR FIRST BORN
I DO NOT   KNOW YOU PETER
WHERE YOU LIE
IN YOUR UNMARKED   GRAVE
HIGH   IN THE HILLS

                    PETER!

I DO NOT   KNOW YOU
OR YOUR FATHER
                DO NOT   DO NOT   WANT TO

DEAR GOD
LET THE NIGHTS
KEEP THEIR   SECRETS'

REGISTRATION OF DEATH / CANADA: PROVINCE OF SASKATCHEWAN

to the memory of peter suknatskyj

　　　　　　　　　　　　　　　　　... on the margins
　　　　　　　　　　　　　　　　　　　　　　　of all things

1. Name of De-
ceased in full
　If an unnamed　　　*Died unnamed*
child give sur-
name preceded
by 'unnamed'.

　　　　　　　　　　　　to hear the cock crow
　　　　　　　　　　　　to be gone
　　　　　　　　　　　　　　　　the third day
　　　　　　　　　　　　　　　　before
　　　　　　　　　　　　　　　　naming
　　　　　　　　　　　　　　　　by water

　　　　　　　　　　　　to not bear
　　　　　　　　　　　　　　　the chosen name

2. Date of death.　　26　　　　day of　*Sept.*　1922

　　　　　　　　　　　　　　　... on the margins
　　　　　　　　　　　　　　　　　　　　of all things

6. Place of Death
　If outside the
limits of a city,　　　*32 · 4 · 2 · W 3*
town or village,
give sec., tp.
and rge.

83

                to lie under
                        mantling darkness
                                        like a sin marked
                        by the nameless
                                stone
                                        in the NE corner
                                                        of a cemetery
                in the game
                                preserve
                                        where whitetail deer
                                descend
                                        the hills
                spring to fall
                                heads angled
                                                under barbed wire
                                to graze
                                        the tall green
                                                        grass

Remark:
(For Registrar
only)   *Child reported very frail at birth and*
                        died suddenly on 3rd day.

        to be discovered
                        in the charred
                                        records
                flung by the new
                                storekeeper
                        into
                                the nuisance grounds
                                                on the margins
                                of all things
                                        lost

любити, а крім Тебе нічого ін-
шого не бажаю!

Люблю Тебе Ісусе:

Отче наш: Богор. Діво: Слава: І нині:

XIV.
Ісуса Христа вкладають
до гробу.

Величаєм Тя,
животдавче Хри-
сте, І чтем крест
Т в о й честний,
імже спасл єси
н а с от работи
вражія.

Розваж, як ученики несуть мертвого
Спасителя на місце, де мають Його похо-
вати. Многострадальна Мати йде за ними
й власними руками складає Тіло до гробу.
Потім замикають гріб і всі відходять.

Похоронений Ісусе! Я обці-
ловую той камінь, що закрив
Тебе, та по трьох днях Ти вос-

FOUND FRAGMENT

after a letter from margaret laurence

the way   we torture ourselves
is it essential
to register
all births marriages   and deaths?
what better burial
than to lie among poplars
under   that huge blue
blue prairie sky
and is it not sad
that your father   should feel
the weight
of having done something
which was right?
the parents are those   who bury
the dead child
with love and mourning
the baby was *theirs*
and they buried that child
under the poplars
the right   and natural
thing to do
and 'no one knows to this day'
your father said
and why should anyone?
and it's sad   your father

carrying the guilt
of all these years
for not declaring
the child's birth   and death
for not filling out
all the official papers
  'there will be others'
he said   comfortingly
so right
and so wrong
there *were* others
but they never replace
the lost one
gone forever
and i think both your parents
knew this   but they
will never be able
to say it
you have these words
and will

88

SUKNATSKYJ ADDRESSING A SECOND UNCLE

uncle   they say you always got anything
you wanted
you know uncle   had you been caught
you would have surely received
the requisite   number of lashes
but women then   were far too afraid
ever to speak

i am grateful   never to have known you
except your faceless name
in my memory
where sometimes
another strawstuffed doll
drifts up   to my mother's face
at christmas time
my father leering

   'herrez a nyce von   live too
    on eet eesn't even
    heez'

somewhere deep   in my memory
a potbellied heater
and severed doll's straw bodies
burn forever
kindling the thought
of all those   julian calender christmases
straw rustling   under the tablecloth

GODDAMN
GODDAMN YOU UNCLE!
may maggots evolve into high order consuming
your live bones   uncle
if we all rise someday
as some say we will
don't you ever cross my path
in these sad prairie hills
because i'll club you
with a femur bone   into still
another   boneshattering
death

заслуги болю, який Ти витерпів при здираню з Тебе одежі, прошу Тебе, поможи мені позбутися всякого привязання до річей сотворених і цілою моєю волею прилягнути до Тебе, бо тільки Ти найгідніший моєї любови.

Люблю Тебе Ісусе:

Отче наш: Богор. Діво: Слава: І нині:

XI.
Ісуса Христа прибивають до хреста.

Величаєм Тя, животдавче Христе, і чтем крест Твой честний, імже спасл єси нас от работи вражія.

Розваж, як кати кидають Ісуса на хрест, а Він з розпростертими раменами прино-

13th april friday good it's not a
how weeks many shock since electricity now
long treatment passed my through brain
they how will be it form can till I
than more a day sentences two?

November 27, 1958

Above mentioned patient was seen for the first time
on Oct. 24, 1958, at the psychiatric O.P.D. of the
St. Boniface Hospital.

She appeared unclean, untidy, apparently unable
to look after herself. Although she was fairly
co-operative she refused to be hospitalized for
'multiple sclerosis,' in 1956.

saturday bells winnipeg of them loved i use to
who wonder lives now in room that to left top at
of stairway north kildonan house that
sister pauline to walked st boniface daily
from hospital 40 blocks stolen with food for me
more 40 blocks to back walk that winter ...
in the end did why i never that door open?
made me what cruel so when her loved i most?
food by left door cold she and often crying
sitting few moments that stairway on to
warm up before home going ... write in her
as always daily diary

1957 Jan 6th
Today my thoughts fly back
to when I was a little girl
when we celebrated Dad's wilia.
How time does change things.
Tonight he sits alone on the farm
with no one to carole to him,
or even to sit with him.

With the help of Social Service and Welfare
Departments, patient was coaxed to come in on
Nov. 6, 1958. Her neurological findings
displayed ataxic nystagmus, 4 limb pyramidal
tract syndrome, moderate cerebellar disease,
sl. intention tremor and slow scanning
speech. Mentally she was about the same as
on Oct. 24th, when seen at the O.P.D. she
was well oriented, her memory seemed
unaffected although occasionally she seemed
incredible. There was no psychotic symptom.
Her mood was somewhat flattened. At times
she giggled and behaved in a silly way.
Generally she displayed some euphoria.

why do they treat us this way? why do we have to
leave these crumbling walls, and
go out into the city on week days, to scrub and
polish floors for prominent doctors — all for
nothing? and here ... why can these sane young
men, who are suppose to be caring for us, take us
anytime they wish? and do whatever they please.
i remember that day, them behind the divider —
their groans, and her young muffled voice. did
they really believe, they could erase it from
her memory with electricity the next day? today,
i must write a letter.

dear mom & andrei

it's so lonely in here. it's so long since
anyone has come to see me. they don't give us
very much to eat in here. metro, could you
please send me a few apples and oranges?
and maybe a few chocolate bars. my favourite
bar was always cuban lunch.

> *love,*
> *eve*

p.s. mom, please pray for me. pray i will
*   get better.*

Patient's greatest problem was her addiction
to Equanil and her wish to have a job. She was
discharged on Nov. 20th, 1958, placed on
Sparine and promised to appear regularly
at the O.P.D.

After a few days however, it was reported
by the Social Services Department that
patient apparently had slipped back into
her habit and was unable to look after herself.

as a small girl, my life began shelling peas from the garden
on the farm. now, it ends shelling peas again. me seated
on the hard green chair. these hands once held the needle
or a patient's wrist. my face once resembling a beautiful
serene nun. my face now like some escarpment crumbling
into a river. joy now the light in the eyes of the baby
crawling between thin feet of the young girl who helps
me shell these chrisly peas. the baby was born here last
christmas eve.

Since she is not co-operative, it is necessary
to institutionalize this patient.

Yours truly,

Wolfgang Helm, M.D.
Assistant Resident
in Psychiatry

it ends with this. hydroemiclysis. i am no longer fed
intravenously. long needles inserted
directly into me – my world now,
pure oxygen, crystal memory, a tent. all sounds
and voices still there, clear as the sharp ring
of a coin falling on stone.

'eve, can you hear me now?
mom took the greyhound from
moose jaw last night.
the village took up a collection
for the fare. she's coming
to see you ... eve'

of course i can hear you sister. but how can i tell you now mostly one lee soparlo speaking

now it all begins like this   in primal meaning of name
suknatskyj namesake   listener on margins
of linage   hero   yearning to make it true
suknatskyj   carder and weaver   of carpathian wool
to clothe comrade   in war
suknatskyj   who questions the very earth   others stand on
calling it theirs   that place
mantling his parents   in a single season
there is the whitehooded priest   confirming fears
    'maybe you're right out at the end of the plank,
    all over again, without a fixed voice again ...'
and there is *mahzahkahzah*   clown turning agony
into an absolving joke
    'hey man   that soparlo   he was king man
    back in yer village   that man man
    he became yer memory   you've had yer say man
    give im back iz hills   you kin live somewhere else now ...'
that man   whose perfect roman profile assumes the shadow
vectoring towards   the bar's clock   indicating
three minutes   to closing time   when he says
'now it all begins like this   each day
with the morning parade
yer wearin yellow coveralls   an yer all lined up
three ranks: first   center   an rear
45 guys   to a platoon   an it's rifle inspection
wen the sargent clears   the barbed wire
from iz throat

PORT ARMS!

you remove the mag   from yer rifle
you place yer sloped rifle   at port
yer right foot   extending forward

95

you cock the action   sliding the bolt back
an returning it   five times
then pull the trigger   this uncocks the weapon
you then slide that bolt
back   an leave the chamber open
you lick yer thumbnail   an stick it in the breech
then swing that barrel   straight aheadda you
the sargent peers a second   intta that barrel
that better reflect   the light   yer thumbnail mirrors
face to face   with the sargent   you stare right through im
an wen ee looks away   moves on to the nex man
you close the action   pull the trigger
replace the mag   an slope arms
then you stand at ease
                              ... now during target practice
it's a whole new game   yer rifle   that lee-enfield .303
it has an accuracy range   of 1200 yards
now the flipup peepsight   starting at 300
is marked for every   100 yards
now wen you flip up that backsight   vertical
that peephole   is adjustable
so by way of   loosening a knurled knob
which wen tightened down again   holds the reticule
in place   you kin slide it up
an set it   at say   900 yards
now wen you stare through that peephole
everything'll   grow a tad fuzzy   but in aboutta second
a clear spot'll appear   right in th center
clear as a bell
you take only another second   situating the target
so as to be able to place it   within the sight reticule
and bring it in line   with the blade of the foresight
you then breathe in   drawing that bead   on the silhouette
of a man's head   that pops up   outtova trench
you breathe out   while you
squeeze the trigger

96

YOU GODDDIT!
DEADCENTER!

now that's   only halfa the game
if it's for real
an the wind's blowing   say ten miles per hour
you aim for the man's chest   you consider the windage
then take a lead   about the width of iz body
an that silhouette   ain't gonna be eatin
no more apples ...'

                    OKAY PEOPLE! CLOSIN TIME
                    DRINK UP! LET'S ALL GO HOME
                    CLOSIN TIME ...

and when the lights are out
there is still the needling question   of that man who became
memory   he still telling you stories
their power prevailing   to change you
when already acolytes   to the mercurial word
urge you to move on   wary of
unwavering faith   in language   choosing you
while voices bear gifts   for the worthy
betrayer   knowing his lot
there is still the nuzzling question   of earth
you stand on   claim
but you know you must   move on
shouldering   into strong wind   at night
where you light   no more than two matches
per cigarette
taking heed   among friends
and lighting no more   than two cigarettes
with one match
the flame   the eternal ghost gun uses
to draw a bead ...

'I promise you I won't die
on opening day....'
                    Robert Raurk

gallagher cleans it yearly now
reverently draws the rod and oiled gauze
through the barrel
a light rag seems to move at its own will
polishing dark blue steel till it gleams
like a hint of memory drawn
from dark past
gallagher finally polishes the walnut stalk
till the ghost gun mirrors
his face

opening day of upland
when gallagher points his station wagon south
down number 14
and takes the first long pull of *calgary* ale
eternally nestled in his crotch
the ghost gun is always there now
snug in its case
lying on the back seat where the other gun
leans angled
                    and he knows it isn't easy
hunting alone now
where a lonely straying thought creases
the flowering black spot
at 11 o'clock

... now you remember son
the way da hunt huns is yeh gotta form
this mental image ovva partridge
in yer mind's eye   an then
yeh transfer it   to that stubble
you stop the car son
shut the motor off
                    ... and you listen
    you wait till that weed or clod
    grows a beak   an the head
    shifts its angle   slightly
    yeh know what to do after that ... son

sometimes on the timeburnished margins of memory
when gallagher is on foot
along the edge of rosehip cover
that suddenly explodes with grouse
he will draw a bead on one
lead it an imaginary bird   or two
depending on the wind
it is mostly then someone seems always there
at the blurred edge of vision
one good eye squinting
the *over and under* in life the ghost gun
deadrings for
                in the hands of he whom
gallagher mirrors dropping
a perfect double
everytime
                a covey flies in tight
                ... formation

99

FARM DOGS

bill hanowski remembering

yeh well   like i say
we couldn't raise enough dogs
to keep up with the horses
kicking them to death
most of them   would run behind a horse
an snap at its feet   like i say
they would just bark   an bite the hind feet
until a horse   would catch one of them   with a hoof
an that   would be the end of that dog
some of them   just never learned
others   became good farm dogs   learned to snap
an then duck low
so the horse kicked over their heads
yeh well   like they say
'a dog's a man's best friend'
he'll follow you anywhere
but that's the trouble
you got to watch them
leave your dog at home   tied up
when you go to the field
i had one once   that followed me
where i was swathing
got chasing a rabbit   and i lost sight of them
the rabbit   did a somersault
ass overteakettle   on the canvas
an my dog lost   all four feet
in the blade
best dog   i ever had
yeah well   like i said before
'a dog's your best friend'
but you got to be careful   at harvest time
or when you hay

the other janitors   are throwing away christmas trees
that brightened   government waiting rooms
for the last three weeks
tonight is ukrainian christmas eve
suknatskyj decides to leave his tree   for one more day
the tree's thirteen gingerbread men   gazing across partitions
an acre of welfare offices
and he is haunted by thoughts of the ukrainian baker's dozen
thirteen gingerbread men
reminding him of   his father's mother
who sold eggs and bread buns   by the dozen
thirteen items carefully packed   each time
the one bun   or egg extra
a gift   for good luck

near midnight   the work completed in suknatskyj's area
he pilfers   one gingerbread man
remembers   an ancient ukrainian custom
when his family always left something
out on the table   overnight
after the dishes were cleared away
the table cloth straightened   over its fine layer
of grass   or straw
remembers how his family   always believed
some relative   would return
from the dead   and stand there   savour something
and listen   for voices   of past christmases
remembers how his mother said
the spirit   must never go hungry
and always left   a small piece of white fish
the northern fisherman sold   to the villagers
each winter   and how she placed
a spoonful   of *kutia*   in a small dish
that sweet   boiled wheat
like some signature   of her scattered family

ole bill hanowski   and suknatskyj wait
for the rest to be through
stand by the table   in the book repository
suknatskyj pulling the gingerbreadman   from a pocket
asks hanowski
   'you remember   the old custom   bill?
   that leavin somethin behind   for some spirit
   after ukrainian christmas eve   supper?
   i stole this one   from my tree
   still up in welfare   tonight'
suknatskyj then breaks off   the head
with raisin eyes   hands it to the old man
who smiles   takes it
an wistfully   murmurs
    'yup   well?
    like i said before
    those were the good times
    it's all different   now'

suknatskyj perplexed
  what sort of ukie drinks tea
  reading the saturday globe and mail
  down in the depot café?

suknatskyj deep in art theory
and national consciousness

  'The fact that Harris
  believes in the spiritual
  energies of the world
  were beamed southward
  from a source at the top
  of the world'

at the edge of suknatskyj's vision
an old man   in a brown fur coat
nearly reaching his ankles
wears a fur cap
with flaps   partly covering his ears
he holds a small box
under one arm
and a tray with a bowl of soup
bun   and butter
in the other hand

he sits down at the table   right of suknatskyj
gently places   the cardboard box
in the middle of the table
then removes the food
from the tray

  and that Canada,
  being closer to

'nice day today   cold
good day forr dha sleep
put bottle homebrew   underr pillow
wake up   drrink few ounces
go back to sleep!'

suknatskyj stirring   back to life
from his newspaper
                          'yeh   tz'okay
                          where you from?'

'arrboorg!   farr norrt!'

                          'what's your name?'
                                    suknatskyj shameless

'ahntohny thorrne'

                          'but you have
                          a slavic accent!'

'yah   tohny toporosky
vahz *rreal* name
eenglishmenz shorrten it   dhey say
ahntohny thorrne shorrterr
easierr to rememberr'

    the source, would
    eventually surpass
    America in the arts
    and culture ...'

suknatskyj curious
                    'you in town just for the day?'

'no   *herre von veek now*'
tony nudges the box   to his right
and rubs his fingers
one by one
'lohking forr job'

                    'how old are you tony?'

'64   *get pension*
in von morre yearr'

'that's admirable tony
lookin for a job
when so few   young people
can find anything   today
knowing there's no where   to go'

the soup finished
tony   picks up his small box
rising to leave
while suknatskyj also rises
both walking to the doorway   and out
to the waiting room   for local departures
suknatskyj finally asking

          'do you think you'll get a job?'

'oh   i look round nudderr veek
hehv to mehk sohme mohney   to get hohme'

          'where's arburg?'

'farr norrt   farr norrt!'

          'how far?   what's the fare
          by bus cost?'

'mahbe   hundrred milsh!
farre? $4. 10'

          'if you don't get a job
          how will you get home?'

tony lifts his box   a bit higher
under his right arm
'oh   peek few cohke bohttlez'

          'if you had the money
          would you take the next bus?'

'oh yes   i goh rright now'

a bus idling outside
suknatskyj slips a blue bill
from his pocket

> *'here's your fare tony*
> *tz'bin nice talkin to you*
> *… tz's good day   for sleep*
> *whiskey under the pillow'*

'yah yah!   good!
tehnkyou   i got bohttle at home!'

tony   places his box
on the chair   walks directly to
the ticketwindow

'von vay to arrburg
please   sehrr!'

106

waiting for the next flight
suknatskyj reads *the tribune*   and *the free press*
till the announcement   unsettles him

BECAUSE OF STORM CONDITIONS
IN EASTERN CANADA
AIRCANADA FLT 620
WILL NOW ARRIVE AT 10:00 PM

suknatskyj fuming   turns to st sanka
even reads a stray *midnight magazine*
left on some lonely seat

finally   the plane taxies towards the runway
eternity glimmering on the burnished
aluminum nose

TAKE   OFF!

the city dropping in sheer moments
like the trap door   of a scaffold
suknatskyj musing

   down there friday night beer   and whiskey
   flow as peaceful   as the red river
   under ice
                   where will it all end
           this flight into   oblivion?

an hour later   the plane touches down
in saskatoon

ARRIVAL!

subzero night threatens   to crack
suknatskyj's face in   half
at the edge of *departures*
where he flags a taxi
suknatskyj warm in taxi
delights in the driver's first words
the rolled r's   welcome as home
'you must be russian   or ukrainian
what's your name?'

   'ukrainian   andrei fedak jr'

'hey! that's amazing!
i'm andrei suknatskyj jr
we both have our fathers' names'

the older andrei murmuring
   'my fatherr   1926
   he went to eenglish forreman
   want get job mit rrailrroad crrew
   building trrack to churrchill
   forreman say
                  'andrei fedak
                  that's be name too tohff
                  forr payrroll keeperr
                  we give you nice eenglish name
                  you worrk mit us
                  lottsa ukrainians herre
                  father say
                  'BULLSHIT! UNGLEEKEE!
                  STICK JOB UP YOURR ASS
                  NO JOB   WORRTH MY NAME!'

   so he went homesteading   in 1928
   nearr dauphin manitoba'

old andrei tells how his wife   left him
20 years ago   and how he had one lung removed
6 years later
  'was the left one
    that cushions the hearrt'

                    remembers the doctor telling him
                    'you have only four years
                    even less   if you continue to work
                    i suggest welfare'
                    'bullshit! if i stop worrking
                    i die   frrom purre borredom!'

he tells of continuing to smoke
a pack of *players* a day
and having never felt better
while he drives a taxi   14 years now
since he quit carpentry
tells how he and his wife   bear no illwill
toward each other
still spending each christmas   and easter
together   at the oldest daughter's home
in winnipeg
claims it's never been better
  'we neverr got divorrced   no need to
    we neverr took up   mit anyone else'

tells of nearly going blind
while studying the bible   after his wife left
he figuring things out   for himself
  'those *gideon* people
    they pirrated worrd   frrom us
    when we always talked about the old men
    we say
        '*ti didi*
          those didos …

well those eenglishmen   magpie thiefs
they stole worrdd frrom us
call theirr bible forr salesmen
gideons!'

 suknatskyj curious
"andrei   tell me about *ukraina*
'ukraine   motherland'
didn't taras shevchenko   first use the word
in a poem?"
metro wincing
   "no   was taras bulba!
   you see   it firrst mean

          that place   wherre you was look out frrom
          that place   surrounded by
          otherr places   ukraina!
          otherr people   otherr countrries
          rround us
          like worrd ohliadaty
                    '*to go look arround*'
                    same mit ukraina
                    be in one place
                    look rround at otherrs
                    we all getting along
                    speaking sevrral languages
                    an   how you call it?
                    survive ..."

suknatskyj suddenly suggesting
'eclectics   we're the eclectics!
weave the spirit   and other things
together ... like combed   *konopli*!*
that kievan centre   an the frontier lands
the cossaks rode to
                    like a carpenter's plumb line
                    hanging perfectly
                    in our memory   of all things
                    east   an west ...

    'rright!'

    metro drops suknatskyj off   downtown
    where he catches a bus
    to the city's eastern edge

* Ukrainian for 'hemp'.

III

three of us walking the empty street   where the bus is parked
we enjoy the silence   and fresh evening air
while the driver   has another coffee
before carnduff   the end of his route

finally the old woman   in a babushka
protecting her   from the flowering cold
stands beside   the coke machine   by the depot
while i edge over   closer
to ask her   how far she's going

   'i going bienfait   spen tenksgeeving dare
    veet ole veedo fren'

i tell her
'i'm going there myself?'

   'you knoh peeplee dare?'

'no   i'm just going there
to find someone who can tell me
about the three miners
who were shot   during the estevan riot   of 31'

   'oh ...'

   she says quietly
   turning slightly   away from me
   in the cooling silence
   to gaze into the southern sky
   where dark clouds
   knowing no country   drift south
   through her evening dream

once it was harry bronfman's liquor warehouse
when locals drove souped up hacks nightly
south into north dakota
where gunny sacks of overproof booze   were unloaded
logging chains magically dropped
from beneath black bumpers
pluming dust a quarter mile high
to blind RCMP cars
but those times are only   a withered memory
today is thanksgiving
and it's 9 AM   as retired miners wait
for alex ronyk   to open the door
so the gin rummy for dimes and quarters
can begin

ronyk resembling a friendly alligator
soon arrives   to open the door
and shortly   four men are seated   at an old table
covered with faded green felt
cards shuffled   and dealt
it all begins again   with laughter   and gentle curses
growing till an old buck shouts   to a skinny oletimer
  'PUMP ME UP!

            PUMP ME UP!

                    YOU OLE PISSCUTTER!'

loud laughter is lost in the rafters
ronyk pothers around the counter
where i lean with one arm   to ask him
about the place   he muses
'yeah   it's a good pastime   for the ole boys
loota fullas here ain't missed a game
since i opened in 35   after quiting the mine'

laughter rises   while the fat man kids   a small wizened guy
who like some pheasant   crouches lower
leaning into the game

'*baniak   baniak**   you ole fucker!
   you're tighter than hogan's goat!'
baniak   only smiles
a perfect smile
squeezing his
cards
into a tighter
fan ...

ronyk remembers the old mining days
when he was only a kid   in 1912
taking care of horses   in the stable
deep underground
'it was spring   the year i started
but then so what   we never saw the seasons go by   anyway
we got up before the sun   and came home after sunset'

at the table   more insults
   'judge   you ole fart
   you bin sittin on your cards   you ole fucker!'
while someone counts up the points
   '*tak samo   tak samo*   this also'
ronyk digressing   from memories of the mine
says
'ole judge   he's bin among us so long
he even talks ukrainian now'

while the men eye me suspiciously
i lower my voice   not to alter the game
ask ronyk in our common language
about three men murdered in 31
and the way   to the cemetery
'*kuda tzvyntar   de spochyvaint
ti try zamordovani khlopy?*'

   '*bez streku*   "over the railway tracks"'
   he says   with tense quietness
               'most of the others
               are there by now'

baniak: Ukrainian for cooking pot.

114

MIKE KALAPAKA'S POOLHALL

alvena   saskatchewan
last night   old man kalapaka
fitted new felt   on the snooker table   near windows
light brown felt   something
suknatskyj's   never seen

  'much cheaper   these days
   green's too expensive   anyway
   ain't too much business here anymore'

kalapaka   and some young french man   run a fast game
fast for the young guy   in early forties
who still believes   he has somewhere to go
in the next ten minutes
kalapaka   casually   pauses
carefully plans   each shot

beyond the shiny worn   barber chair
men   even older than kalapaca
sit in the bright light   near the window
and watch   the way they've watched   others play
20?   30?   40 years?
deep breath   held
kalapaka   sinks
another perfect   8 ball
in the far   corner

vasylyna
      retreating into wilderness
                had it

     po vukha!
     'to the ears'

          with people
vasylyna
      perfectly able
          building herself
      adobe house
          with straw roof

vasylyna
      constructing
          a simple shelter
      of shakes
          and scrap lumber
              for a goat
         one milk cow
            and a few chickens

      arrive alone
          on the margins
              of vasylyna's
        poplars
          and the ghostly
     flatbreasted
        figure
          with a doublebarrel shotgun
     delicately
        angled
          across the right shoulder
     will call

     KHTO TAM?
     'WHO GOES THERE'

and failing to answer
                    in vasylyna's language
                                        or going
          any further
                    can only end
          in feet
                    e x p l o d i n g
                                beneath one

              though vasylyna's gun
                              has never been
                                              fired
                    in fifty years

but go there
              with mykola
                            if you ever find him
              and vasylyna
                            will make tea
                                        and reveal
              unspeakable things
                                in translation

              '... do you know
              the englishmen
              they are snakes!
              sometimes   i fry them
              in my frying pan! yes!

              ... and the frenchmen
              they are   dogs! yes!
              i keep them tied
              in the poplars! yes!

              ... do you know   last night
              there was a mist
              Jesus Christ   and i
              we flew high above vita!

                    children   would you care
                    for some more tea?'

noonhour suknatskyj
                a mouth upon him
                        for hot soup
        suknatskyj fawning
                over the menu

'nah honey!
we got nah clamcahdeh tahday
jis soupahdahday honey…'

        'well wahddabout these three soups here?
        chicken noodle
                split pea
                        an this here borshch?
        kin i have some borshch?'

'well we dowen really call thadda soup honeh!'

        'tzokay okay with me
        i'll have some'

an eternity later
                manhattan borshch arrives
a scoop
        of sour cream
                with a generous handful of
        finely chopped
                beets floating around
        … suspiciously
                no suggestive steam wafting up
        to commingle
                deliciously
                      with hint
        of dill

suknatskyj
        uneasily stirs it all
                muses
                   where
      are my broad beans
              tasting of prairie earth?

        stirs that dollop
                of sour cream
      becoming a dozen
             hopeless islands
                  something
     reminiscent of ice floes
             in a sea
                of thin
        raspberry juice!

flatfaced suknatskyj
        takes a tentative spoonful
                to tease
      tastebuds
        'UGH!
          ICECOLD!
         MANHATTAN
             BORSHCH!'

cornercafé mamma
      casually explaining
'well honeh
     maybe some *jewish* place
heats it up
bahddats the way we shevvit heeh ... honeh!
             ICECOLD!
      reeefrrrehshin! onna hot
      new yok day'

ukrainian sound poem in spring (for sonia sorestad)

viter vüe
viter vüe
     wind blowing
     wind blowing
     wind blowing
     wind blowing
          viter vüe
          viter vüe
             H U R A K A N !

         kan
         kan
            gone cities
         kan
         kan
            gone the trees
         kan
         kan
           gone

2. ZHURAVLI

zhuravli
zhuravli
     letiat
     letiat
     letiat

cranes flying
cranes flying
zhuravli
     letiat
         bez mriaku
         bez mriaku
         de vsio posypaietsia iak
         popil
         popil
            nad selom

cranes flying
    flying through mist
        through mist
            where all floats like
            ashes
            ashes
                over the village

dukh
dukh
do nykh
    letyt
    letyt
    krychyt

the spirit
    spirit
        flies out to them
        flies out to them

                zori
                zori

de vony
    letiat
    letiat
        i krychat
            biz svit
            biz nas
            biz svit
            biz nas
            biz smert!

to them
        village lights are stars
                stars
                stars
                      where they fly
                          fly
                              and cry
                                    over earth
                                    over us
                                    over earth
                                    over us
                                    over death

3. LIOMPA

lioom paaah
lioom paaah
lioom paaah
        oom paaah
        oom paaah
        oom paaah
                paaah
                paaah
                      moroz vlizaie v kosti
                      frost creeps into bone
dusha vidlitala
        allah
        allah
        allah
                the soul
                      has fled

adaptation after anon. ukrainian song
as remembered by michael demjanew of winnipeg

kokain
kukulu
kokain
liquor from *kukulu*
ah how i love to drink you

for you i give all
silver and gold
and in return
you give me sleep
in the soft cold mud

kokain
kukulu
kokain
kukulu

lying down i sleep
like a bull calf
and when i waken
the day is pure white

kokain
kukulu
kokain
kukulu

returning home
i weep walking slow
and often rest
then finally run

kokain
kukulu
kokain
kukulu

for you i sweat like the dew
grow old grow old
all too soon
kokain kukulu

kokain kukulu
i *need* you
for you i give all
silver and gold

kokain
kukulu
kokain
kukulu

* '*Kokain*' ukrainian for cocaine and a special poppy plant from which some
say ukrainians, back in the old country, brewed a kind of ukrainian 'white-
lightning'. others say it was *kokil*: a weed with black seeds growing wild. i
imagine *kukulu* was a word the first singer generated for his kokain-tongue-
tied dream of home.

TABLE OF CONTENTS